Tyson's Treasure

By Cameron Macintosh

Illustrated by Adam Nickel

Pearson Australia
(a division of Pearson Australia Group Pty Ltd)
707 Collins Street, Melbourne, Victoria 3008
PO Box 23360, Melbourne, Victoria 8012
www.pearson.com.au

First published 2010 by Pearson Australia
2019 2018 2017 2016
10 9 8 7 6 5 4 3 2

Publisher: Simone Calderwood
Illustrator: Adam Nickel
Editors: Lisa Warden and Sophie Ayerbe
Designer: Jennifer Johnston
Copyright & Pictures Editor: Helen Mammides
Project Editor: Aisling Coughlan
Production Controller: Claire Henry
Printed in Australia by the SOS Print + Media Group

ISBN 978 1 4425 2810 9

Pearson Australia Group Pty Ltd ABN 40 004 245 943

Contents

Chapter 1

A Phone Comes Calling

Last Sunday already seems so long ago. So much has happened since then, I feel like I've just come back from a family holiday on Neptune.

It started off like any other Sunday. There I was, sitting in my room putting my dog back together. Marvin had been in another fight with next door's Labra-bot. A tangle of green and red wires was hanging loose where his back leg was meant to be.

I was trying to keep him still when Mum burst into the room, grinning like she'd just won the Laser Lotto. "Tyson, this is amazing!" she yelled. "I finally found one in the bottom of a junk pod!"

I looked up from Marvin's messy leg socket. Cradled in Mum's hand was a small silver device with a rectangular screen and a number pad. An antique mobile phone— I'd seen Mum sell stacks of those things in her shop.

I shrugged. "What's so special about that?"

"This one's 207 years old," said Mum, "and... *and*... it's got a battery!"

A battery! All of a sudden, this was different. These days, batteries are even harder to find than old toothbrushes.

I did some backwards counting. It's 2210, so minus 207 years—that would mean the phone was made in 2003. The oldest phone we'd ever had in the shop was a 2010 model, and that one sold for a fortune.

Mum made enough money from the sale to buy me and Sophie new FlyPods.

She even had enough left over to put new air-conditioners in the shop and in our home above it. All that from a phone that had no battery. The more I thought about Mum's latest find, the more excited I got.

I love Mum's shop and the funny old stuff she sells, but it hasn't been the same since we lost Dad two years ago.

And things had been getting harder already, thanks to the Collectamax Corporation. They'd opened their first Melbourne megastore the year before, selling a much bigger range of old things than Mum could ever find by herself—and selling them cheaper, too. But, with a bit of help from me and my sister Sophie, she's hanging in.

Last week, Mum sold two cameras that were made back in 2016. They still worked, but they could only take photos in 2-D—talk about boring! She also sold a 1988 muesli bar and a big batch of credit cards from the 1990s that someone wanted to use for kitchen tiles. All of that made Mum pretty happy, but we both knew it was nothing compared to what a 2003 phone with a real 2003 battery would sell for.

I asked Mum for a closer look, and she carefully handed it over. It was covered in scratches and the numbers were almost worn off, but for such an old phone it was in pretty good shape.

Except, of course, that it probably hadn't worked for about 200 years.

Someone rang the buzzer down in the shop, so Mum hurried out of the room. "Put it in the safety pod when you've finished, dear!" she called back to me.

I turned the phone over in my hand and slid the back off. I'd never seen a phone battery before. It didn't look like anything special, but I knew what a difference it would make for Mum. People would line up around the block to see a real phone battery… and plenty of phone collectors would pay almost anything to make it theirs.

I was just about to take the phone downstairs to the safety pod when Marvin started jumping around and blipping furiously. He seemed to think I'd spent too much time looking at the phone and not enough time reattaching his leg.

Then I felt a sharp bump on my hand and before I knew it, Marvin was rolling on the floor with the phone in his mouth. I nearly fainted on the spot. Marvin's a toothless beagletron, but his jaws are like a vice—if he decided to really chomp down, he could crush an old phone in a millisecond. There was only one thing to do—jump on top of him and push his power button.

Beagletrons aren't soft to land on. They aren't exactly placid either. Even with a leg missing, Marvin rolled across the floor as if an eleven-year-old boy wasn't clinging like mad to his back.

We bounced and tumbled around the room until finally my fingers found Marvin's power button. He froze immediately, like an icicle. I heard a clunk, and saw the phone lying on the floor in one piece, safe and sound—it was a miracle.

But something had changed. The screen was glowing now, a faint blue colour. My heart nearly leapt out of my mouth when I picked it up and saw a bunch of words slowly forming on the screen:

WELCOME TO
RAPTUS TELECOM

Chapter 2

The PIN Puzzle

Now it was me grinning like I'd won the Laser Lotto. A 2003 mobile phone with a battery—a battery that actually works—in 2210, that's like finding fifty buried treasures at once.

But when I looked down at the phone again, the smile dropped off my face. The words on the screen had changed to something else:

ENTER PIN

PIN? That must have been one of those weird twenty-first century things. I flipped up the antenna behind my left ear and looked down at my palm. Then, I said two words, right into the middle of my hand:

"Define PIN."

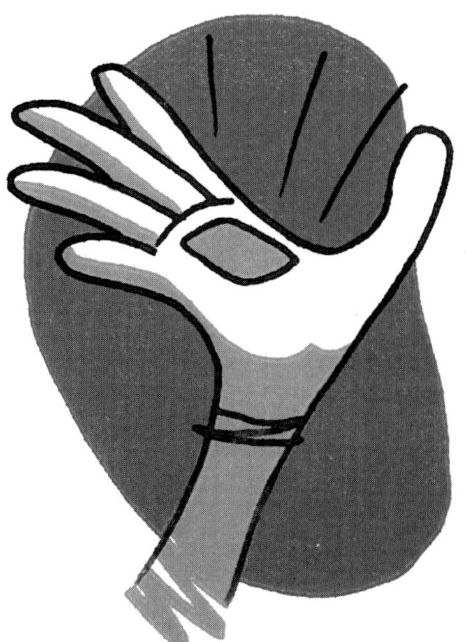

My palm glowed white and filled up with words. The first sentence told me all about sewing pins, the second about bowling pins. Not very helpful. But the last line of text at the bottom of my palm read:

PIN: Personal Identification Number. Before tongue-print technology, PINs were a security feature of many electronic devices.

I flipped my antenna down and my palm faded back to skin colour. The Global Mindweb had saved the day once again.

From what I could gather, I had to enter a four-digit PIN to make the phone actually work—if it did actually work. It made sense to start off with 0000 and work my way up. As soon as I punched it in, the phone replied with a nasty message:

PIN incorrect

Hmmm, I thought. *This could take a while.*

I tried 0001 and got the same message, but things got really messy when I tapped in 0002. This time I got a different message:

Security violation.
Phone locked. Enter
unlock code.

This was going to be a challenge, but thank goodness the Global Mindweb was there to help.

I flipped my antenna back up, and asked for information about 2003 mobile phone security violations.

A few minutes later, I was entering an unlock code. Believe it or not, the code actually worked—the phone unlocked and asked me for the PIN again. Right away, I tapped in 0003 and imagined the commotion when we told the world we'd found an ancient phone that could still make calls. This was getting more exciting by the second!

Chapter 3

Ancient Messages

It happened at 9.45 p.m. I was sitting up in bed, keying in digits. Marvin was on the floor, licking his leg wires and looking at me like I'd forgotten something.

My fingers were tired from button pushing, and I was starting to worry about the phone's battery. When I switched it on the first time, there were five full battery bars. I was already down to four bars, just from tapping in PINs.

I'd worked my way up to 7461. By now, it wasn't just my fingers that were getting tired. But then I tapped in 7462 and the screen said:

PIN accepted

Suddenly I was more awake than I'd ever been before. This was incredible—no-one had seen this kind of phone menu for almost two centuries!

The menu screen wasn't much to look at, but maybe they didn't really care about those sorts of things back then.

I scrolled down to the item on the menu that said "Messages". Selecting that gave me two options: "Inbox" and "Outbox". Here was the biggest shock of all—there were still real text messages in each of them—200-year-old messages!

I opened the outbox first—maybe it would give me an idea whose phone this had been, all those years ago. There were four messages in there. They were all sent to the same person, someone by the name of BRODIE B.

I scrolled down to the oldest message. The owner had sent it on 5 December 2003:

M8, in sum troub.
Need your help.

I went back to the inbox and scrolled down to the oldest message there. It looked like Brodie B had written back straightaway:

Wots up, nick?

Nick, whoever he was, wrote back a minute later:

Whole case bks fallen
off trk. All in yarra
nr princ brdg. Cant get
em out.

Brodie's reply started with a smiley face—he obviously found the whole thing pretty funny.

☺ R U jokin? U R in deep. Sounds like bks R 2!!

Nick wrote back:

Not funny. They R in plastic wrap but I cant get em out w/o diving in and towin em out. No time 4 that.

Brodie's next text message included a sad face:

Tell your boss they wr stolen. Lv em there. Not much i cn do 2 help. Sorry nicko ☹

Nick replied:

U R right, will say thats wot happnd. Thx 4 that!

The conversation ended with this one from Brodie:

Gd luck m8!

I flicked through the messages again. They made no sense at all. Why all those numbers and shortened words? I really needed some kind of translator, so—you guessed it—I flicked my antenna up and asked the Global Mindweb for help.

Chapter 4

The Marvellous Mindweb

When the Internet melted down in 2036, the Global Mindweb took over completely. Faster, smarter and heaps more fun, it's still the world's most reliable source of information.

But just when I needed it most, I flicked my antenna up and my palm showed nothing but skin. Without the Mindweb, I had no hope of translating those messages, so I switched the phone off to save the battery. Right away, my palm started glowing like it was meant to.

I switched the phone back on, but as soon as I'd tapped in the PIN, my palm went back to skin again. There seemed to be a pattern here…

I switched the phone off and asked the Mindweb for information about twenty-first century mobiles. It told me that these types of phones had been banned in 2037 because of the way they interfered with the entire Mindweb system. *Ah-ha*!

Then, I asked for information about twenty-first century text messages. My palm filled up with options. The one that excited me most was the "Twenty-first Century Digital Abbreviation Converter". I opened it up and tapped into my palm some of the strange things I'd seen in Nick's phone. First one: "M8".

M8 = mate.
An old-fashioned word meaning "friend", commonly used until the late 2090s.

Okay then, how about "troub"? Answer: "trouble". I probably could've worked that one out myself, but this way was a lot more fun.

When I tapped in "bks", things suddenly went from just fun to unbelievably exciting—the converter gave "books" as the most likely translation. When I read that, I felt like an army of spiders was running up my spine. Was Nick telling Brodie he'd dropped a whole case of books into the Yarra River?

The only time I'd ever seen a real book was in the city museum, sealed in an airless, temperature-controlled display case. Mum took me to see it a few years ago. She explained that people used to read and write on a material called paper, until it was banned in 2106 because of all the trees that had to be cut down to make it.

Mum had always dreamed of finding a real book, but she knew there was more chance of finding diamonds on the footpath.

I turned the phone back on and scrolled through the messages until I came to:

All in yarra nr princ brdg.

I didn't need the Mindweb to tell me what "brdg" meant, but "princ brdg"? Did it mean Prince Bridge? Princess Bridge? Princeton Bridge? As far as I knew, there were no bridges by any of those names in Melbourne.

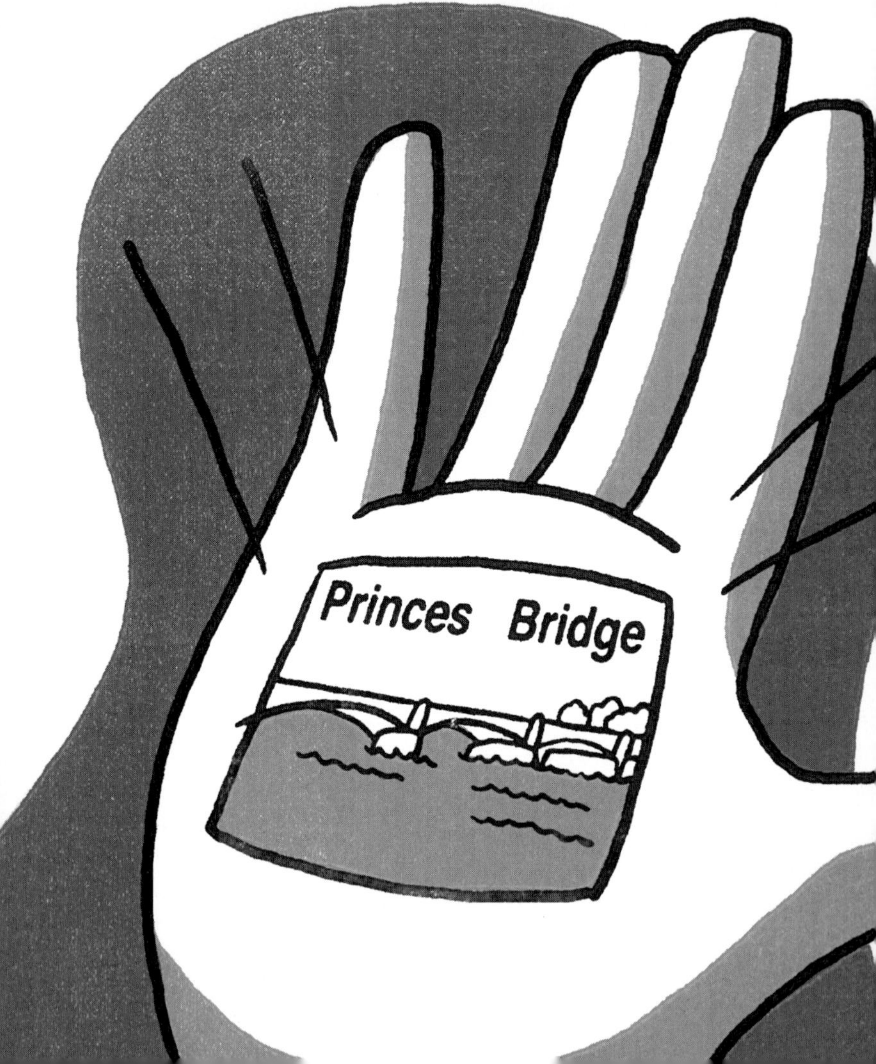

I switched the phone off again and did a Mindweb search on the history of bridges over the Yarra River. According to the Mindweb, in 2003 there'd been seven bridges that crossed the Yarra in central Melbourne. Amazingly enough, one of them was called Princes Bridge. Since 2055, it's been known as the Minogue Overpass—renamed after a singer who'd become Australia's first president. That had to be it, but surely a case of books couldn't survive 200 years in the Yarra, no matter what they were wrapped in ... or could they?

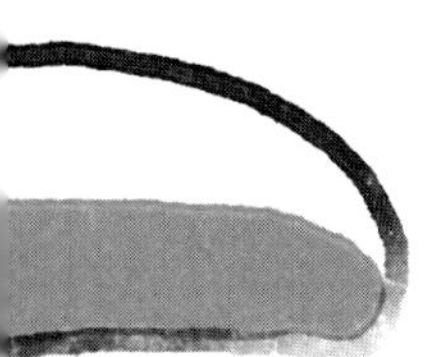

Chapter 5

Riverbed Roving

Although Mum bought us new FlyPods when she sold the 2010 mobile a few years ago, mine's already due for an upgrade. It's zippy enough, but it's useless for towing, or flying any higher than about sixty metres. Still, it was one of the first ones on the market that could both fly and submerge. Last Sunday night, I wouldn't have swapped it for anything.

I reached the Minogue Overpass at 10.45 p.m. It's a beautiful bridge, and one of the city's oldest. Before everyone swapped their cars for FlyPods in the 2190s, it was one of the city's busiest bridges, too. Now it's little more than a pedestrian bridge. These days, if you want to see the traffic, you look upwards. At some times of day, you'd think there was a huge swarm of wasps in the sky. But—luckily for me—at 10.45 p.m. on a Sunday night, things were pretty quiet up there.

As I hovered beside the bridge, I switched my headlights to full beam. Then, I slowly dropped down into the dark, murky waters. It was like sinking into a tar pit, and when I aimed my headlights down at the riverbed I could see what looked like 400 years' worth of junk, covered by a thick layer of brown silt. That was a bit scary—what if there was 200 years' worth of junk on top of Nick's book delivery?

Luckily, as I got closer to the riverbed, the blast from the FlyPod's engine churned up the water and blew the silt away.

The junk on the riverbed seemed to come to life as the brown silt disappeared and revealed whatever colour happened to be beneath it. It was an amazing transformation, but after twenty minutes I still hadn't seen anything that looked like a case of books.

I was about to call it a night when I glided over a big square lump that didn't change colour. I moved the FlyPod closer. The lump still didn't change colour. Whatever it was, it was wrapped in thick plastic the colour of silt. I nudged it with the side of my FlyPod. It didn't budge. Then I got as close as I could and looked at the plastic wrapping. In tiny letters all over it I could see three incredible words:

BERTRAND'S
BOOK SUPPLIES

I don't need to tell you what those three words did to my stomach. Straightaway, I opened out the FlyPod's tow claws and clamped them around the case. Then I pulled the up lever towards the sky.

The case rose up a few centimetres and my engine growled like an angry lion. I pulled the up lever as high as it would go and the growl got louder, but I couldn't get the case more than five or six centimetres off the riverbed. I kept trying, but the engine started squealing and the up lever started shaking like a jackhammer. It was time to try something else. I lowered the case back to the riverbed and retracted the tow claws.

Then I noticed something that made me gasp in horror. Tiny bubbles were seeping out of a small tear in the plastic. With my heart pounding like a thousand bongos, I rushed upwards and homewards as fast as the angry engine could carry me, leaving the precious case behind.

Chapter 6

The Soggiest, Soppiest Story

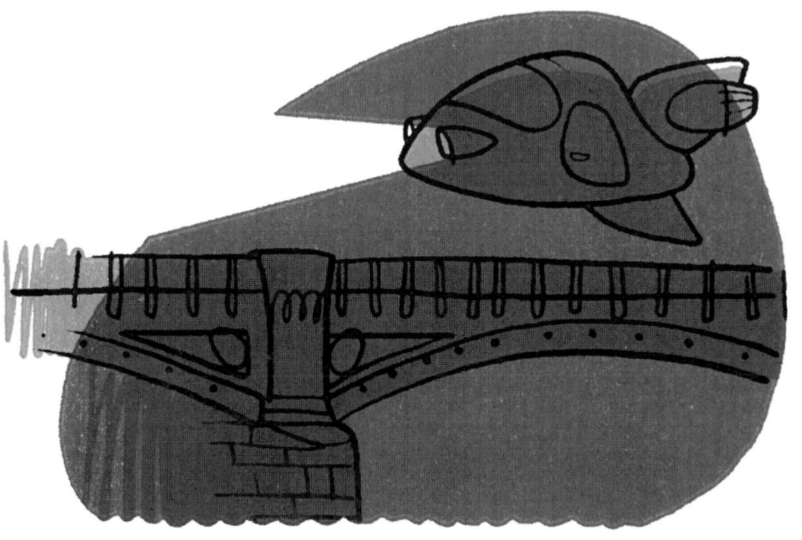

It's lucky that Sophie, my sister, is a heavy sleeper. If she had heard me zooming off into the night in her new F66 FlyPodMax, she'd probably have strangled me. But this was urgent—I needed a high-powered FlyPod, and Sophie had just won a new one last week in a game of robo-bingo. I wasn't going to waste time asking for her permission.

By the time I got back to the Overpass, the surface of the river above the case was frothing like a spa bath. I plunged Sophie's FlyPodMax straight in and down to the bottom. My heart sank when I saw how fast the bubbles were spewing out of the case.

I pushed out the FlyPodMax's tow claws and clamped them around the case as carefully as I could. Then, I took a deep breath and pulled the up lever.

The FlyPodMax lifted the case as if it was as light as an empty shoebox. Seconds later I was hovering above the river, the case dripping globs of silty water out of the tear in the plastic.

I used the tow claws to lower the case onto the path beside the river, and climbed out of the FlyPodMax. I slashed the plastic open with the ignition key and reached into a gap between two of the planks in the case.

This should have been the greatest moment of my life—but the first book I grabbed fell to pieces in my hand. So did the second, then the third … eighth … twelfth …

they were all just a mess of soggy paper.

It was almost too much to bear.

Book by slimy book, I ploughed through the case, dumping piles of white sludge on the path beside me. And then … I felt it. A handful of dryness, right in the middle of the case. I rubbed my hand on my pants, reached back in and gently pulled it out. I'd never seen anything so amazing. A book—a real, actual, paper book!

By the glow of a streetlight, I could see three words on the cover:

Teresa's Tropical Treasure

and a picture of a sun-kissed couple hugging under a palm tree.

I laughed out loud. This was the kind of soppy story I'd tease Sophie about if I found her reading one on her Digi-book. But the book was well named—it really was treasure. Only a few weeks ago, Mum had told me of a similar book she'd seen at her favourite auction house. That one had been missing some pages but it had still sold for $250 000!

If only I had a time machine, I'd go back 207 years and send a text message of my own:

Thx 4 that, Nick & Brodie B!
IOU big time ☺

Chapter 7

Varley's Valuation

It was two days to Mum's birthday. This time I had a surprise beyond anything she could ever imagine—a surprise that could save her business, and maybe even pay for another family adventure on Neptune.

To make the surprise even better, I decided to find out exactly how much the book was worth. Then, when Mum opened it, I could tell her right then and there how much she could expect to sell it for.

On the way to school on Monday, I paid a visit to Varley's Valuations—a new shop in the city that told people how much their old possessions were worth. I parked my FlyPod outside, pushed open the door and went up to the counter. The book was carefully wrapped in an old T-shirt.

The man behind the counter, who I guessed was Mr Varley, the owner, looked about seventy. He was slouched behind the counter, polishing an old teapot. He didn't even look up when I gave a little cough to get his attention.

"Hello," I said. "I've got something here you might like to look at."

"Mmm-hmm."

"You probably won't have seen too many of these before."

Mr Varley breathed out through his large, round nostrils and kept polishing the teapot as if I wasn't even there.

I started unwrapping the T-shirt from around the book. The second that Mr Varley caught a glimpse of the book cover, his eyes doubled in size and his spine went dead straight. Then he slouched across the counter and let out a long sigh.

"Yes, *Teresa's Tropical Treasure*. We've had quite a few of these through here. Terrible book, but worth a few dollars."

That was what I wanted to hear!

"Around about how many dollars?" I asked.

Mr Varley scratched his chin. "Hmm… a book in good condition like this could probably sell for about… $2000."

I felt the colour drain out of my face. These days you can't even buy a second-hand Labra-bot for $2000. So much for saving Mum's business. I started to wrap the book up again, but Mr Varley stood up and held out his hand.

"Why don't you leave that with me while you're at school," he said. "This kind of paper disintegrates quickly on humid days like today. I'll keep it safe in the conservation vault out back."

I didn't need much convincing. Although $2000 was nowhere near as much as I'd hoped, Mum could still use it to feed us for a few weeks. I handed the book to Mr Varley, thanked him for his help and hurried off to school.

Chapter 8

Worrying Window Shopping

"Tyson!" yelled Ms Moretti. "Less daydreaming, more mind-sculpting."

"Sorry, Ms Moretti." I sighed and turned back to the marble cow I was carving with the school's new mind-sculpting drill.

As you can probably imagine, I had other things on my mind that morning. Mostly I was trying to figure out how such an old book in such good condition could be worth so little.

And there was another thing too—although I didn't want to believe it, something about Mr Varley didn't seem quite right.

When 3.30 p.m. finally came around, I was the first one into the FlyPod shed, and the first one into the afternoon sky.

Varley's Valuations was only a five-minute flight from the school, but the journey felt like five years. Even though I was in such a hurry, I saw something that made me screech to a halt in front of the Collectamax megastore a few doors down from Mr Varley's shop. In a glass case in the main display window was a perfectly preserved copy of *Teresa's Tropical Treasure*. Its price tag was written in gold on a piece of black plastic:

BARGAIN!
Genuine 2003 edition …
classic romance
Only $260 000

I gulped. My stomach did somersaults. I gulped again. And then I sped down the street to Varley's Valuations as fast as my FlyPod could carry me.

When I got there, I felt sick. The front window of the shop was boarded up with old pieces of wood and there was a big

CLOSED

sign on the door. I hammered on it with my fist, but no-one answered.

Seconds later, I was back at Collectamax, standing as tall as I could and demanding to speak to the manager.

"I'm the manager," replied a bearded man behind the counter. "Is there something I can do for you?"

"The book in the window—where did you get it?"

The manager's nostrils flared out in a way that reminded me of…someone, but who? "It's none of your business how I find stock for my store," he said.

"It *is* my business when you're selling a book that belongs to me," I said firmly.

The manager took a step backwards and pressed a button on the wall behind him.

At that moment, the air around me started to fizz. Suddenly I couldn't move my limbs. And then I started sliding backwards across the floor, like my shoes had turned into ice skates. Before I knew it, the door was opening behind me and I was sliding onto the footpath. The door slammed in my face and locked shut with a clang.

Well, that was it. Right away I was back in my FlyPod—and heading towards the nearest police station.

Chapter 9

Whatever It Takes

I could still hear the police officers laughing as I climbed back into my FlyPod. "A book from the bottom of the Yarra… 200 years old… in perfect condition. He's lucky we didn't lock him up!"

I couldn't believe it. The best thing that ever happened to me had turned into the worst. Why did I trust anyone with the book—especially a complete stranger?

That night at the dinner table, Mum and Sophie knew something was up. But I couldn't bring myself to tell them what had happened.

As soon as we finished eating, I stomped up to my room and went back to work on poor Marvin's leg.

Business had been slow lately, and Mum had decided not to sell the 2003 mobile until she'd restored it to mint condition. In the meantime, she couldn't even give me enough pocket money to replace Marvin's torn wires. I had to fuse two old ones together with a laser pen. It took ages, and even when the wires were safely inside Marvin's leg, he still couldn't walk properly.

This just wasn't good enough. We deserved better than this. As Marvin's leg hissed sparks and dropped onto the floor, I decided that, whatever it took, that book was mine, and I was going to get it back. Seconds later, I was in my FlyPod, zooming back to Collectamax as fast as I could.

I arrived at 8.15 p.m. I expected the shop to be closed, but all the lights were on. From out on the street I could see customers wandering around, checking out the ancient computers and video game consoles.

I hurried straight to the display window, and nearly fainted on the footpath—the book was gone! Looking into the shop, I could see where it had gone to. The manager was wearing gloves and flicking through the pages for an elderly couple, who seemed extremely impressed with it.

Taking a deep breath, I ran into the shop, straight towards the counter. The manager saw me coming. Before I knew it, he was reaching for another button on the wall behind him. The second he pressed it, I bounced backwards and landed flat on my back. I jumped up straight away and tried again.

The manager hit another button. This time, my feet stuck to the floor like I'd just stepped in ultra-glue. Then, he picked up his hyper-phone and barked a command: "Southbank Police Department. Here. Now."

I was in trouble, and there was only one person who could get me out of it—Mum. I slid a hand into my pocket and grabbed my hyper-phone. But when I pulled it out, I realised it wasn't my hyper-phone at all. Somehow I'd picked up the 2003 mobile instead. In all the excitement, I'd forgotten to put it in the safety pod. Hopefully it was better than nothing.

I switched it on and tapped in the PIN—and felt my feet suddenly detach from the floor.

It looked like the Global Mindweb wasn't the only thing the phone interfered with! Before the manager had finished reporting me to the police, I was out that door, into my FlyPod and on my way home.

Chapter 10

Crashlanding

I look absolutely ridiculous with a moustache. I look even worse with a fibre-optic wig on my head. But wearing both, I look nothing like me. This was extremely handy when I walked back into Collectamax half an hour later.

The book hadn't sold, thank goodness. It was back in the glass case in the window.

The manager didn't notice me walk up to the case and tap the PIN into the old mobile. But he did look up and start yelling when I opened the back of the case, grabbed *Teresa's Tropical Treasure* and tucked it inside my jacket. He frantically pressed his wall buttons, but none of them did anything. I laughed out loud, kissed the old mobile and sprinted out the door.

At first, I thought I'd given him the slip. Then I saw a pair of PolicePods tailing me—and just behind them, a FlyPod with Collectamax logos on it. Things weren't looking good, but that book was mine and I wasn't giving it up without a fight.

I pushed my accelerator to the floor and pulled the up lever as high as it could go. A few seconds later, I was sixty metres above the ground, swinging between buildings and dodging sleepy office workers who were finally on their way home.

But the police were gaining on me. If I couldn't fly over the skyscrapers, they'd catch up in no time.

I yanked the up lever as hard as I could, and the FlyPod creaked. It lifted another couple of metres, then groaned and started drifting downwards like an autumn leaf. The up lever had come completely loose in its socket. I'd really blown it this time.

The other three FlyPods were only metres behind me when I crashed into the footpath. Before I knew it, I was surrounded.

The Collectamax manager sneered at me. "Step out of your vehicle," he snarled through his FlyPod window, "and give the book to the nice police officers."

I locked my exit hatch and tore off the moustache and wig. "No," I said. "*You* step out of *your* vehicle and tell the nice officers how this book ended up in your store. Otherwise, you'll be getting it back in a million little pieces."

"You don't mean that," he said. But when I held the cover with both hands, like I was about to tear it, his face turned the colour of beetroot.

He charged towards me in his FlyPod, but I stopped him in his tracks by making a tearing noise with my tongue. He pulled to a halt, begging me to stop and whimpering like a puppy.

POLICE

COLLECTA

The Collectamax manager looked so ridiculous, begging like that, I couldn't help laughing. Even the police officers seemed to find it all a bit funny.

Just then, I remembered the old mobile. I pulled it out of my pocket and scrolled through the menu to the text messages. "This," I said to the police officers, "might be of interest to you."

The police officers were amazed when I showed them the conversation between Nick and Brodie B. The manager didn't say a word, but he did start whimpering again when I told the police that he looked an awful lot like the Mr Varley who'd tricked me into handing over the book.

The police officers asked him to tug on his beard, and that was the last straw. He pulled on his up lever and shot up towards the sky like a bullet.

"Well, that book seems to be yours," said one of the officers. "Our friend up there has a bit of explaining to do."

Sirens screeching, the officers rocketed upwards, gaining on Mr Varley so quickly that I knew he didn't stand a chance.

Relieved and exhausted, I hugged the book like a long-lost friend, and headed straight for home.

Chapter 11

The Fantastic Future

As you can probably imagine, Mum's birthday this year was the best since...well, since we had Dad around. Mum couldn't stop hugging me, and just this once, neither could Sophie. But Marvin seemed to be the happiest of all of us. With four working legs, he spent the whole night somersaulting around the living room.

After all the excitement died down, Mum took the book to a real valuer, and learned that it was worth about 200 times more than Mr Varley had suggested. What's more, the city museum was more than happy to pay her the full value.

Teresa's Tropical Treasure now sits in a temperature-controlled display case next to a telephone from the 1960s and an electric guitar (with real strings!) from the 1990s.

As for me and my family, the money from the book certainly saved our business, but it hasn't changed us at all. We're still on the hunt for a perfect 2010 MP3 player, and a well-preserved 2020 bi-sky-cycle.

And, of course, we're always on the lookout for books, too—the soppier the better. Who knows, maybe one day there'll be enough trees again for someone to make a real book about us!